Mistakes Help Us Learn

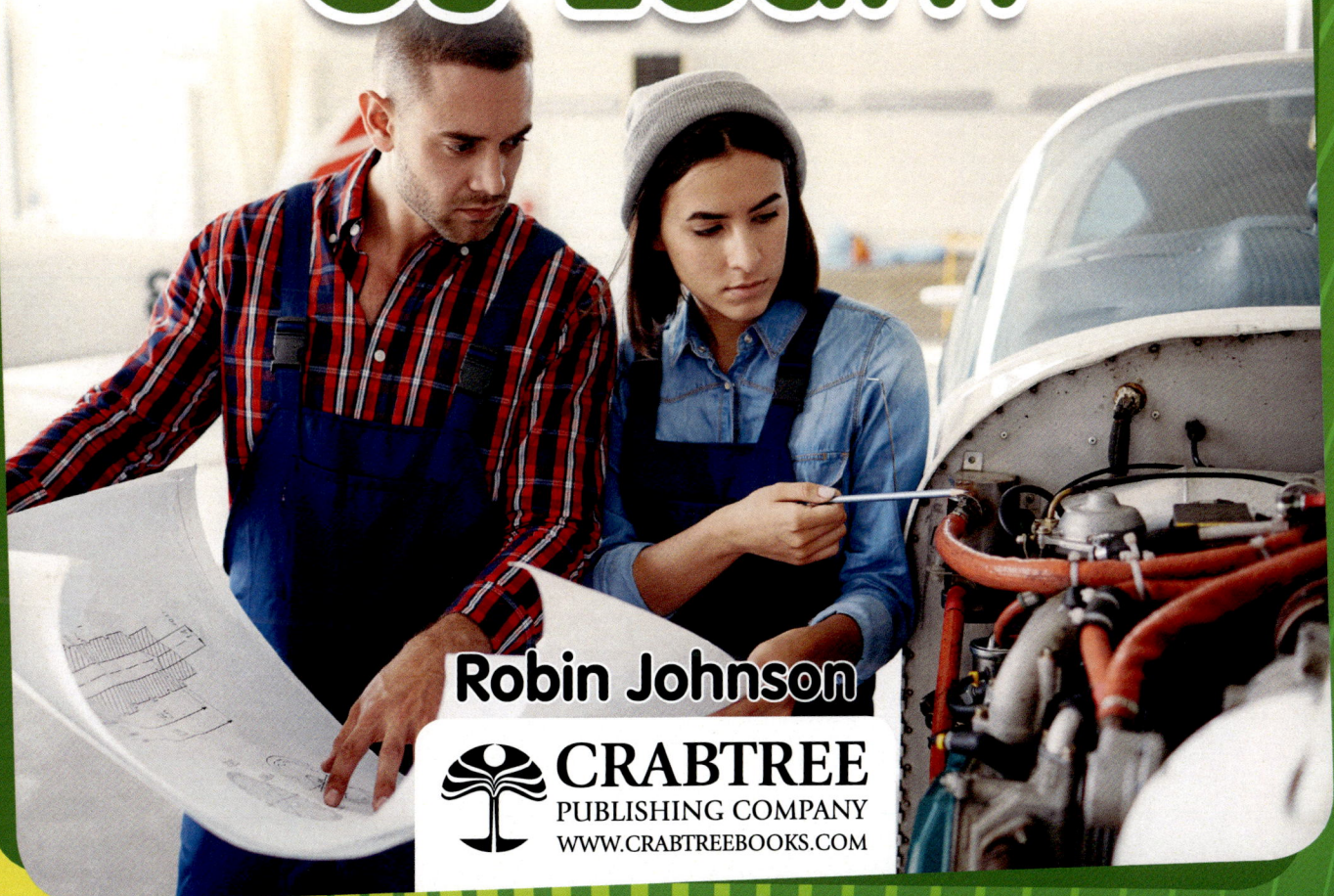

Robin Johnson

CRABTREE
PUBLISHING COMPANY
WWW.CRABTREEBOOKS.COM

Title-Specific Learning Objectives:

Readers will:

- Describe the steps engineers take to design solutions.
- Understand that engineers welcome and learn from mistakes, and that mistakes are a chance to learn.
- Identify main ideas in the book and explain the reasons the author gives to support the ideas.

High-frequency words (grade one) a, and, are, do, is, not, of, their, they, to, with	Academic vocabulary artificial, creative thinking, design, improve, invented, model, solution

Before, During, and After Reading Prompts:

Activate Prior Knowledge and Make Predictions:

Have children read the title and look at the cover and title-page images.

- How are mistakes positive things?
- Have you made a mistake that helped you learn how to improve?
- Why do you think it might be important for engineers to learn from mistakes?

During Reading:

After reading pages 8 and 9, ask:

- What do you notice about the word model? (It is in bold type.) Show children the definition of model on page 22. Remind them that the glossary is a tool they can use while they read.
- Return to pages 8 and 9. Ask children to explain why models are important to engineers, and restate the idea on the spread in their own words.

After Reading:

Have children discuss the main idea of the book: mistakes help engineers learn. Encourage children to make text-to-self connections by describing ways that mistakes help them learn. Have children draw a picture of a time that they learned from a mistake. Create posters titled "Mistakes Help Us Learn!" that display the pictures.

Author: Robin Johnson

Series Development: Reagan Miller

Editor: Janine Deschenes

Proofreader: Melissa Boyce

STEAM Notes for Educators: Janine Deschenes

Guided Reading Leveling: Publishing Solutions Group

Cover, Interior Design, and Prepress: Samara Parent

Photo research: Samara Parent

Production coordinator: Katherine Berti

Photographs:
Getty images: Sergei Bobylev: p. 11; David Levenson: p. 19; Westend61: p. 21
Public Domain: p. 15 (bottom)
Shutterstock: joyfuldesigns: p. 14
All other photographs by Shutterstock

Library and Archives Canada Cataloguing in Publication

Johnson, Robin (Robin R.), author
        Mistakes help us learn / Robin Johnson.

(Full STEAM ahead!)
Includes index.
Issued in print and electronic formats.
ISBN 978-0-7787-6207-2 (hardcover).--
ISBN 978-0-7787-6252-2 (softcover).--ISBN 978-1-4271-2263-6 (HTML)

        1. System failures (Engineering)--Juvenile literature. 2. Engineering design--Juvenile literature. 3. Engineers--Juvenile literature. 4. Problem solving--Juvenile literature. I. Title.

TA169.5.J64 2019   j620'.00452   C2018-906191-X
                                                                          C2018-906192-8

Library of Congress Cataloging-in-Publication Data

Names: Johnson, Robin (Robin R.) author.
Title: Mistakes help us learn / Robin Johnson.
Description: New York, New York : Crabtree Publishing Company, [2019] | Series: Full STEAM ahead! | Includes index.
Identifiers: LCCN 2018056593 (print) | LCCN 2018059497 (ebook) | ISBN 9781427122636 (Electronic) | ISBN 9780778762072 (hardcover : alk. paper) | ISBN 9780778762522 (pbk. : alk. paper)
Subjects: LCSH: System failures (Engineering)--Juvenile literature. | Experiential learning--Juvenile literature. | Continuous improvement--Juvenile literature.
Classification: LCC TA169.5 (ebook) | LCC TA169.5 .J64 2019 (print) | DDC 620/.00452--dc23
LC record available at https://lccn.loc.gov/2018056593

Printed in Canada/022022/CPC20220214

Table of Contents

Crabtree Publishing Company

www.crabtreebooks.com   1-800-387-7650

Copyright © **2019 CRABTREE PUBLISHING COMPANY.** All rights reserved. No part of this publication may be reproduced, stored in a retrieval system or be transmitted in any form or by any means, electronic, mechanical, photocopying, recording, or otherwise, without the prior written permission of Crabtree Publishing Company. In Canada: We acknowledge the financial support of the Government of Canada through the Book Publishing Industry Development Program (BPIDP) for our publishing activities.

Published in Canada
Crabtree Publishing
616 Welland Ave.
St. Catharines, Ontario
L2M 5V6

Published in the United States
Crabtree Publishing
PMB 59051
350 Fifth Avenue, 59th Floor
New York, New York 10118

Published in the United Kingdom
Crabtree Publishing
Maritime House
Basin Road North, Hove
BN41 1WR

Published in Australia
Crabtree Publishing
Unit 3 – 5 Currumbin Court
Capalaba
QLD 4157

A Chance to Learn

People are problem solvers. They find ways to make life easier, safer, and more fun. But **solutions** do not always work the first time. Making mistakes is part of problem solving. Every mistake is a chance to learn.

People often work together to solve problems.

These friends are building a tower. The first tower they built fell down. So, they stacked the blocks a different way. Now, the tower stands tall! They learned from their mistake.

Engineers Solve Problems

Engineers are people who use math, science, and **creative thinking** to solve problems. Engineers know that making mistakes is a chance to learn.

Engineers enjoy solving problems, even if they make mistakes.

Learning from mistakes helps engineers **design** better solutions. Roads are safer today because engineers have learned from mistakes in the past.

Testing One, Two, Three

When engineers have an idea for a solution, they make a **model**. Then, they test it. Testing lets them see if their idea solves the problem.

Engineers make careful plans when they design solutions. But they do not always get it right the first time.

Testing models helps engineers find mistakes.
Then, they can fix the mistakes.

This engineer is making a model of a car.
He will test it and look for mistakes.
Then, he will fix the mistakes.

Keep Trying

If their model does not solve the problem, engineers do not give up. They learn what went wrong. Then, they **improve** their design.

Engineers can change the size or shape of the solution. They can change what it is made of. They can change how it works.

This girl has an **artificial** hand. Engineers tested the hand many times. They fixed mistakes. Now, her hand works well! She can use it to change the light bulb.

Sharing Mistakes

Engineers share their ideas with each other. They also share their mistakes. Sharing mistakes helps engineers learn and design better solutions.

Engineers make sure others do not make the same mistakes.

Sharing ideas and mistakes can help engineers solve new problems!

Learning From the Past

Engineers also learn from mistakes that people made long ago. They learn why other solutions failed. They make sure they do not make the same mistakes.

An engineer may study a bridge that fell. They learn why it fell. This helps them design safer bridges.

Some engineers study ships that sank, such as the Titanic.
They learn from past mistakes to design stronger, safer ships.

The Titanic
sank in
1912.

Never Give Up!

Engineers may have to change their designs many times. But they do not give up! They learn what went wrong. They use what they learn to make the next design better.

Thomas Edison **invented** the first light bulb. He tried thousands of designs before he found one that worked. How would we light our homes if Thomas Edison had given up?

Amazing Engineering

Learning from mistakes is a big part of designing amazing solutions. Some of the solutions people use every day came from engineers who did not give up.

Have you ever flown in an airplane? It took Orville and Wilbur Wright many years to invent the first airplane. They tested and improved many models.

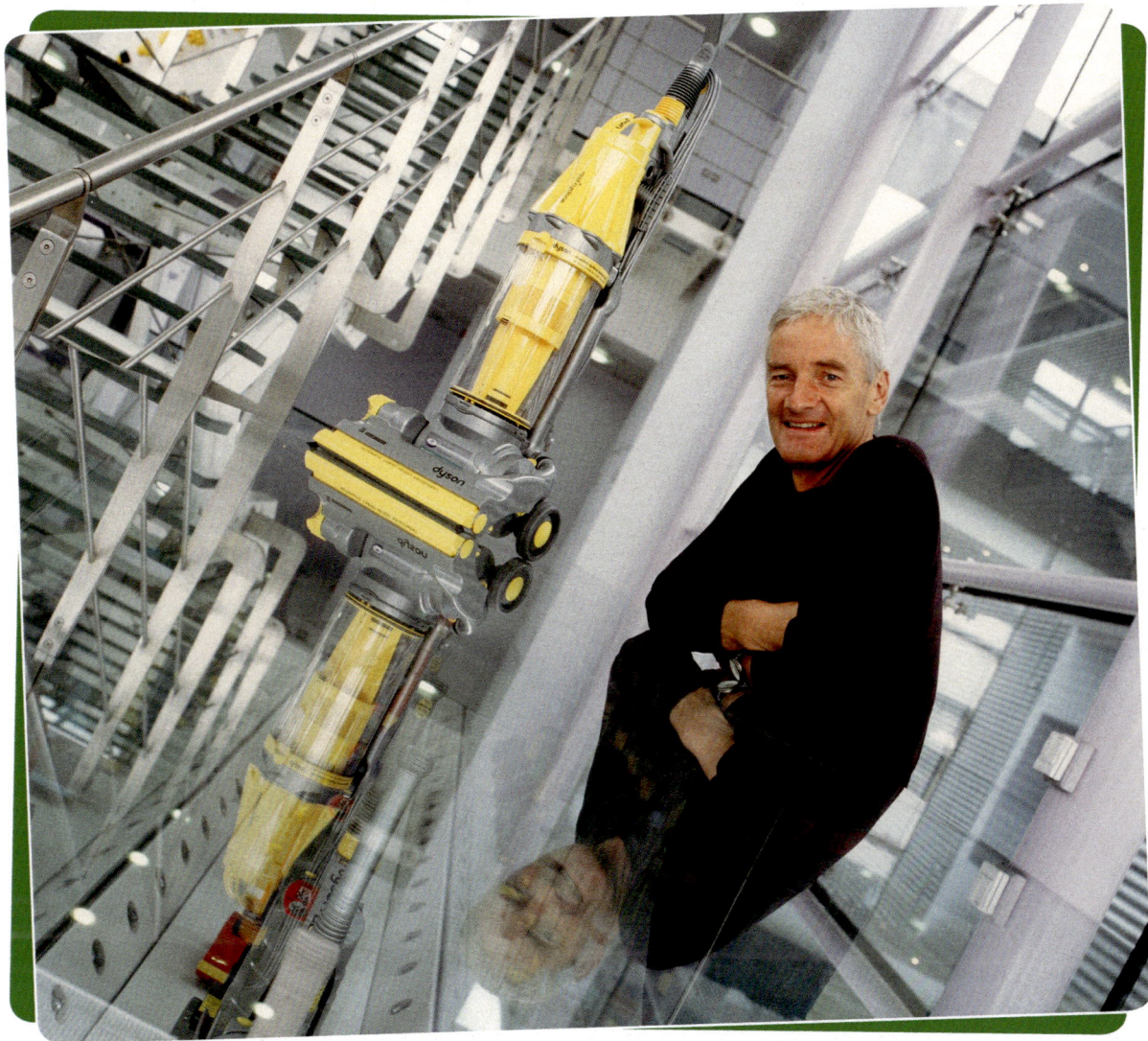

James Dyson designed a new **vacuum cleaner**. He made more than 5,000 models! He kept testing and changing his designs until he got it right. Today, people around the world use his invention.

Always Learning

Engineers know that every mistake helps them learn. Can you think of a time when you learned from a mistake?

This girl made a model of a bridge. She tests it to see if it can hold objects without breaking. After each test, she makes her bridge stronger.

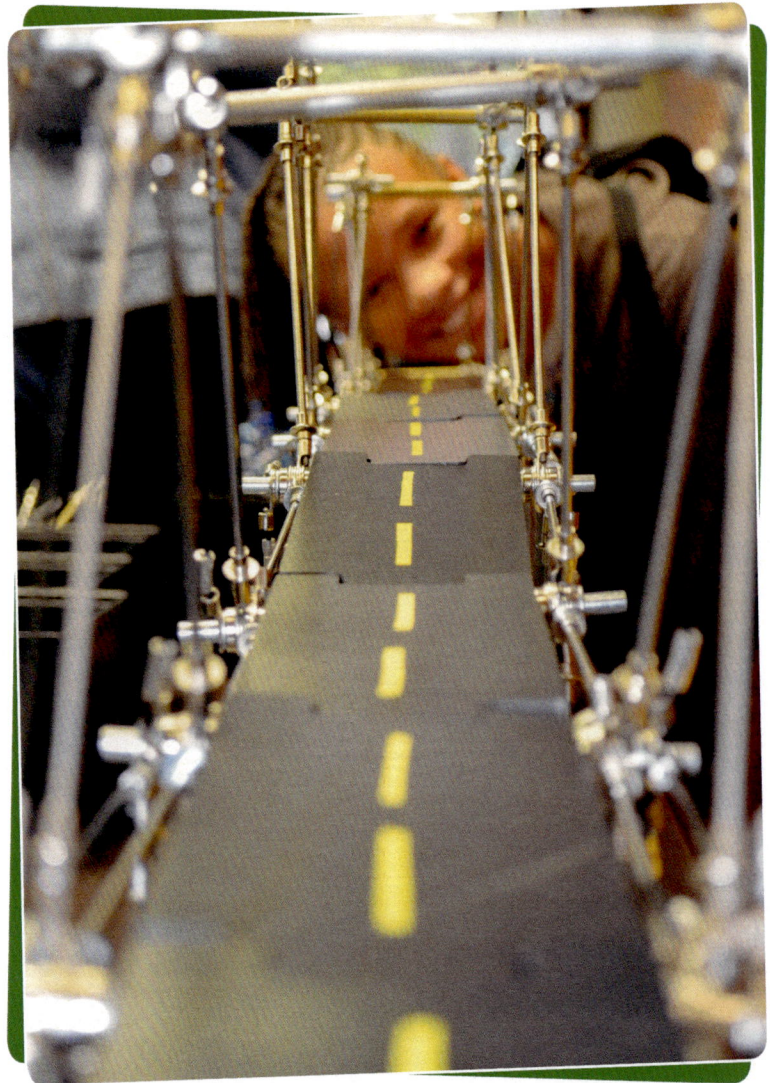

This engineer designed a robot to make cookies. She made and tested many models. Now, her robot makes the cookies just right! What could you design?

Words to Know

artificial [ahr-tuh-FISH-uhl] adjective Made by humans

creative thinking [kree-EY-tiv THING-king] noun Using your mind to make up new and original ideas

design [dih-ZAHYN] verb To make a plan for how something is made or built

improve [im-PROOV] verb To make better

invented [in-VENT-ed] verb Created or thought of something new

model [MOD-l] noun A representation or copy of a real object

solution [suh-LOO-shuhn] noun An answer to a problem

vacuum cleaner [VAK-yoom KLEE-ner] noun A device used to suck up dirt from carpet or floors

A noun is a person, place, or thing.

A verb is an action word that tells you what someone or something does.

An adjective is a word that tells you what something is like.

Index

About the Author

Robin Johnson is a freelance author and editor who has written more than 80 children's books. When she isn't working, Robin builds castles in the sky with her engineer husband and their two best creations—sons Jeremy and Drew.

To explore and learn more, enter the code at the Crabtree Plus website below.

www.crabtreeplus.com/fullsteamahead

Your code is:
fsa20

STEAM Notes for Educators

Full STEAM Ahead is a literacy series that helps readers build vocabulary, fluency, and comprehension while learning about big ideas in STEAM subjects. *Mistakes Help Us Learn* uses cause-and-effect language and clear examples to help readers identify main ideas and the reasons that support those ideas. The STEAM activity below helps readers extend the ideas in the book to build their skills in engineering and language arts.

Building Growth Mindset

Children will be able to:
- Explain why mistakes are an important part of the engineering design process.
- Identify growth mindset, use it to complete an engineering challenge, and reflect on it.

Materials
- Mindset Sorting Chart
- Engineering Challenge Sheet
- My Growth Mindset Sheet
- Buckets and water
- Materials for project, including paper, craft sticks, cardboard, glue, tape, paper rolls, etc.

Guiding Prompts
After reading *Mistakes Help Us Learn*, ask:
- What is a model? Why do engineers make models?
- Why is it important for engineers to test models?
- Why are mistakes an important part of designing solutions?
- Do engineers give up? Why not?

Activity Prompts
Explain to children that "never giving up" is important in engineering—and in all parts of life! Tell children that when we learn from mistakes and do not give up, it is called "growth mindset."

To illustrate, hand each child a Mindset Sorting Chart. As a group, sort the statements in the chart, identifying which are growth statements and which are not (these are called "fixed").

Tell children that they will use growth mindsets to complete a challenge. When they make a mistake, they need to use statements like the ones on their charts to help them keep trying.

In groups of three to four, children will complete the engineering challenge. Hand each group the Engineering Challenge Sheet. Give children one full class period to try the challenge. It is okay if they do not succeed in the end.

Have each child write a reflection on the My Growth Mindset Sheet. Display the reflection responses in the room to showcase the growth mindset of the children.

Extensions
- Have children write a "growth mindset story" and perform it for their peers.

To view and download the worksheets, visit **www.crabtreebooks.com/resources/ printables** or **www.crabtreeplus.com/ fullsteamahead** and enter the code **fsa20**.